The Wesleyan Poetry Program: Volume 63

BETWEEN TWO LIVES

Between
Two
Lives

By

FREDERICK TURNER

WESLEYAN UNIVERSITY PRESS

Middletown, Connecticut

8/1972
Am. Lit. Con

Acknowledgement is gratefully made to Christopher Books and The Unicorn Press, the publishers of three chapbooks in which a number of the poems in this book were first published, and to the journals *Spectrum* and *Tractor*.

Library of Congress Cataloging in Publication Data

Turner, Frederick, 1943-
    Between two lives.

    (The Wesleyan poetry program, v. 63)
    I. Title.
PS3570.U69B4   811'.5'4   72-3726
ISBN 0-8195-2063-2
ISBN 0-8195-1063-7 (pbk.)

Manufactured in the United States of America
First edition

Contents

Deep-Sea Fish : 11

The Ajax Power-Man : 12

Oxfordshire Countryside, 1966 : 14

The Old Black Convertible : 15

Poem : 17

To Sylvia Plath : 22

Chicago Summer : 23

Santa Barbara, 1970 : 24

The Rainy Day : 25

The Process : 27

Birth of a First Son : 29

The Riots, 1968-1969 : 33

The Third World War : 37

Two Poems : 42

The Birds : 43

Reflections : 48

Conversations: for Ben Nelson : 50

The Garden of Eden : 53

Portrait of the Artist : 54

The Water World : 55

The Music : 58

Tochter aus Elysium : 60

The Actor to the Audience : 65

The Proposal : 67

The Cave : 69

In Venice : 73

The Frontiersman : 76

The Search for Tom and Lucy : 79

Libbard's Last Case : 83

BETWEEN TWO LIVES

Deep-Sea Fish

What if we should withdraw from the ocean
A terrible fish, yellow and black
With poison spines and half-tissues
Of slime adhering, and eyes not
Yet formed, blind from the cavernous darks?
Would we still bless the monster?
Would there be pity as you crushed its bony skull
With your heel? Such beasts can only feel
Pain, and they have no delights
As we can see in the holy dolphin
Dancing in heraldic and ecstatic frieze.
Poor beast, having only pain to lose
And yet it would cling to the slow death
Of five metric tons of pressure to the square inch
Because it was a slow death only.
As you crushed its slipping flank
Perhaps the soft milt of its
Defiance of complete annihilation
Would spout from its poor belly in
Pathetic imitation of the lordly whale.
Yet once examined we could not set it free
For its blood even would be bitter toxin
To the legitimate and sporting game that we hunt;
And all its belly's burst, and its
Segmented spine is bent and broken
By the pressures in its blood and sperm
Required to equal those satanic rigours
Of the bottom of the sea.
This devil we have drawn up
Will not let us go unless we bless
And bestow what kindness we can feel upon it.

The Ajax Power-Man

I'd like to be an Ajax Power-man.
Children would follow me; I'd sit on garden walls
With little girls upon my knee, and tell them tales
Of ancient wars with darkness and the beast
Of Dirt, that haunts the working class.
I'd let them hide behind my curlèd cloak
Smoothing their hands on its ineffable and bold
Fabric, white as silk and slick as nylon.
And then one day the van I drove
Would stop upon some moonlit crag
Between a town and village, and I'd take
My powers in both fists, and fly
With subtle gifts inside a sack;
Rebel against the Company, be sought by men with guns
Hunting the wraith that travels at noonday
And night with antique robes aflutter
Like scented wings of angels, or the musky
Pinions of the phoenix, soaring with stolen premiums
And offers of wristwatches, punchbowls of crystal,
Radios and ornaments of sandalwood, bangles and beads.
By day vicars with field-glasses would pick me out
Marking me by the giant 'A' upon my breast;
And, nightly, radar screens would see a ghost
And jets would roar like sullen tides to seek me out.
I'd visit little widows with gifts of satin slippers
Leaping through their windows while they crowed aloud with
    joy;
I'd slink through teenage bedrooms, with necklaces, and rings
Of real jewels, and leave in babies' cots
Rattles of ivory, and tiny sapphire toys.
People would bless me as I passed.

And then at last they'd catch me, bring me down
Like some proud eagle in his flight
And gather round the broken bird that lies upon the ground
Fallen from what clouds and thermals, what towers
Of golden cumulus, bloodstained and superb.
The greatest Power-man of all is dead, they'd say,
Almost a little shamed by what they'd done;
And wrap me in my robes like a magician
And bury me in hallowed ground,
The people's gifts about my head and feet.

Oxfordshire Countryside, 1966

The air is rich cream poured out at evening.
Even the willows over the river glow
With the buttermilk nightfall; the deep grass
Deep as tumbler full of green sweet wine
Is bound and embroidered with buttercups'
Gaudy enamel.

This is a sinister growth.
The acreage of man is not tamed
But warmed with the flesh of dead sweethearts
Strong with the muscles of buried ploughmen.
The forest on the hill is not made
Of antiseptic pines and nordic fir
But beats slowly with the rhythm of a thousand summers
And the soil has known many harvests
Like the warm body of an amorous woman.

The safest land is also the most perilous.
The ghosts of Romans from the villa downstream
Float like the rich rivermists over the meadow
And the swift stream speaks with the slow speech
Of many Saxons with their persistent mind.
We must be protected against history
By the cool smell of petrol, and the metal
Of cars' walls, the accuracy of instruments.
This land is too passionate.
We are always a little frightened
By that which is full and forever
Just as we find it difficult
To peer at the great red sun.

The Old Black Convertible

It was an old black convertible without much left
on the clutch, in a summer afternoon, later
becoming evening in a way one doesn't watch
some year in Oxfordshire, on a particular day

with a friend driving, and three girls in the back,
running through the green fields brushed like mink with
sunlight yellow guard-hairs, and the flowers
in hedgerows singing like a record of polyphony
in an old house, in a part of the country
I never found again, a day

that was all blue and ochre and many tender greens
ending up in a churchyard about teatime
and still hot, supernaturally so for England,
and I remember a ruined farmhouse and
a well, and an almshouse and
the pub we later barged into,

coming home at evening with only a whistle
from the wind, and my face numb, and my
scalp blurred and tired with the wind, and
the tires singing in the dark,
(near dark to the eyes, though green
lingered in the branches of the linden
and the beech, the golden oak in the
blue sky above) me leaning on the
leather of the seat, back, face to the sky, dizzy
and slightly drunk in the hay-smelling
now moonlit and at last yellow dark
river smell and owl and air, still
but moving swiftly as we rush

home, and jokes thrown back in the wind
over the Toad-of-Toad-Hall highway
caught by the girls, nestled now
in female warmth, a trace of
perfume in the eddy, and at last
the turn and crunch of wheels on autumn gravel.

Poem

What a poet is
Is not always a man who suffers
But he who cannot suffer.
Poor god, unable at first
To understand the pain of those he loved.
Only then is the Word spewed out
Mountain-core out of volcano or
Like heart's-blood flowing on the ambulance road.

I am incapable
Of understanding even the effect of my own presence.
Those who stand round see
And I ask them: 'What is the matter with me?
Where is the ugly wound on my body of which I am unaware
But which fixes your attention so?'
But they don't tell me anything.
Perhaps like those who must not be told they are to die
Or those who, already dead, look out
Of curiously coloured and vivid eyes but
Cannot be told anything anymore (or
It is worse, they cannot understand
And think the huge bruise on me's their own);

I am alone
In a volcanic landscape.

'I have a Janus,' said she,
'with two faces, of darkness and light'; lighting a cigarette.
She has a belle heart-shaped face with lips of Apolline
stonecarver's character. As she leans forward and talks the fire
flames in her cheeks, though embarrassment is totally absent
now. She is good company, and we are growing friends.

17

'There are some things in us, very deep down, that we look at sometimes in horror, but which contain the seeds of what we most truly are,' I said. This was purposely vague, for I intended neither to prevent what she was going to say, nor to encourage it. Any compulsion either way could be fairly lethal: like a draught in a perfectly warm room perhaps, but more heartfelt and less aesthetic.

'No, you're right, it's not trivial like picking one's nose or making faces in a mirror. Though the mirror comes into it, I suppose you will say. The fact that I don't happen to be able to get on with men, and incline the other way, could be fairly important.'

'Would you find such a relationship with me, ah, disgusting?' She looked at me with great love in her eyes.

'Yes, that sort of relationship would be disgusting. Don't you see?'

'Of course,' I agreed. 'How difficult it must be to have all that extraordinary love inside you and being able to tell no-one! I remember when I was in love the first time. I walked down the street in the dark under apple blossoms (or mercury lamplight, I'm not sure) and shook hands with everyone I met. I met a distant friend of mine and put my arms around him and said "I love you" to him. He stepped backwards three yards practically into a roadmender's hole.'

'I ran all the way down Broad Street with a plastic rose, looking for black Russian cigarettes. None of the shops had them. It was such a great finding out we both loved the same things and hadn't been able to talk to each other about them, and then we loved each other,' she said; and she was so happy that there were tears pricking like stars in her eyes from the fire.

The dream that she told me:

It is a part of the town where I was a little girl.

There is a sandstone hill ribbed and red,
With the black soot in it, and the church nearby
With a surreal clock clear in the nightmare
Middle distance. These north-country towns
Are often disturbed by unhoused and unlevelled rock
Obscene in its nakedness, quite undeveloped.

There is a canyon ground in the stone
Full of the shadow and round like a river groin
Tall so the skylight is feeble, and smelling of stone.
Here in the daytime I walk, and in terror
I roll myself down so I cannot escape
And there at the end is the light
Of the green haze of a land that is all a sweet chestnut
Standing in summer, by itself, with its candles all pointing
And pointing like Christmas-tree candles, at all of the sky.
There is a joy there I cannot catch.
But in the night I sit in a pub with friends
And drink and even laugh in a conditional way
Back in my home-town, and daren't go into the cave
For it's dark and it's lonely, and I am a woman
And the light that is at its far end, the summer eternal's
Still there, but unseen now: the pub and my friends are enough.
What we desire, perhaps, is too much.

Healthily body must stifle the vapours dark
Of the wicked hot soul, the winds tied up in a bag
The mountain of slag that sits on the magma
The sick cavefuls of fire that must be abated and tamed.
— Though what Freud would say, she chuckled, I'd shudder
   to think.
   She is a poet too, in the special sense that I use the word:
where there's a man who has lost his rhythm and losing it sees
what it is, but cannot regain it again. Not at all a noble

19

experience, productive of bad poetry, like the bad poetry of Hamlet, unformed and perplexed. She is good company.

There was a man who's no longer a friend of mine, for he is becoming a schizophrenic and now I can't reach him. He had a girl all tall and lovely, a woman who might have been a painter's model that created the desire of an age of history: quite unplaceable though, so that one could not say of her 'Quattrocento' or 'Grecoesque'. She was a tower of blond hair and high golden cheeks with a grave and quite gay air that defied the stroke of the man who eventually carved the portrait on her gravestone. My friend was driving. It was November the Fifth, and the spent rockets hung in the leafless trees where the conkers had fallen from; chestnut fingers creaked on the autumn gravel. To get round to it: he was driving, and all of a sudden the car had turned over and now unaccustomed surfaces and edges of it were scoring the tarmac deep. She flew from the passenger seat and fell on her head. So that the neck was broken and she was all soft and a little shapeless inside her dress (but still beautiful in the darkness, pale on the grass verge). She was good company.

I am alone in a volcanic landscape.
Up over Rannoch Moor and past the monstrous deep
Of Loch Ness I have hitch-hiked at night.
And now I am tired and there is a windy silence.
It is the valley that lies behind Coigach
And it is as empty and as dull as a yawn.
Only a few devilish birds must dip and sing
And a river too acid to carry fish
Oozes and tumbles through peat and white stones
From one grey loch to another. There is a smell
That the ice-age left behind, at once musty and sharp
Old as the hills and as new as cruelty.

Long white streamers from the sea
Rise up perpetually from the western moors, and fly
In various shades of violet, to be lost inland,
And over the three great concave peaks that stand
At the head of the valley in purple and grey
Sits a cloud that is full of the rain.

And this one cloud in all the catastrophic sky
Is still, and pours water on the hidden mountaintops.
These are the kings of the valley, the cloud is their mantle.

And now, in a sudden, the hillsides are pouring with falls
So that the churn and crash of it pains the ear
Across all of three miles of empty gulf air.
Such spates are alarming: even the lochs seem to fill
And the valley is full of a crowd of sinister voices.
Yet the note of the waterfalls, once established, does not
    change
One iota, but rises and falls in the ear's fantasy.

I am alone and the earth has been scored
With a malice as slow as the stone, and as old
As a thousand ages of man.

To Sylvia Plath

We are the Adolfs
with our blond spirits, our
Götterdämmerungs, our mastery,
our brutal grip on the rock,
our talk, our talk, our talk;

he with his heavy face,
his slab-sided cheeks, his
Magog shoulders, his overcoat, his genius;
I with my hairy health,
with my also flawed but also
infinitely rayed and expensive jewel:

and you, bitch, vulnerable,
flesh-eater, with your
light mad eyes and ironic,
bitten, hurt mouth, you
selfish self-killer, Janis,
Marilyn, Virginia, Sylvia; Eva Braun;
girl-voice, throat
for strangling, jailbait, prick-teaser,
gasoline virgin; I
cannot stand your sarcasm; I
am violated by the obscene
orgasm of your pyre.

Chicago Summer

An evening of lights; reds and blues; in
a street in Chicago, the Greek quarter, the
heat of the tomcat, furry, gentle drunken night
moist air from the deep gulfs of the Midwest
the steaming gullies, the moist hilltops
a smell of moussaka and chemicals,
perfume and deep wet grass from the plains
the heavy bite of warm ouzo on my palate
like the jaws of an excavator, its shovel
pinions my tongue.

You were afloat
in the same lascivious dream as I;
one was conscious of your brown flesh
under the thick white of your favorite dress. Your
eyes reflected the lights, making them browner
and shiny. Your teeth were white. When
you laughed, I saw into your throat.
You held my hand like a little girl.

In the bar when the dancer came
with the clink! of her brass castanets and
the push of her hip on my breast pocket
you made an experiment in your mind
and felt quite sensual in your light and
furious way. I was lost like a slob in a
heavy relentless fantasy full of thighs. I
wanted to bruise and bite your long fingers, wanted
to breathe the black, midnight
midwest, wet corn cloud of your bushy bright hair.

Santa Barbara, 1970

I wake from an afternoon nap not
knowing who I am
walking out on the terrace, seeing
a strange city, built on the western seaboard of a
continent, under a foreign light of blue
weather one would never expect of a familiar place.

The lights are on before it's dark.
This is not home, this is some minor city of Japan
Provincial coast of France, a Black-Sea town, or
some forgotten port looking on the Galapagos.

I with my moustache, my beard, my flared trousers and
knitted sweater, my unnatural sleeping at noon, my
yawns and my strange thoughts, am
an inhabitant, an
inexplicable local of this foreign land.

The Rainy Day

I feel so sleepy.
It has been raining for four days
the trees are bent deep with
their freight of fresh water.
The skin on my face is tight.
The whole world mourns with
an old little wind blowing by gables.
You can hear a motorcycle in streets far away.
This water epiphany in California
is all those winters in England when
the weeds were sodden with
the wet and the darkness came early
and the shops opened late on Thursday mornings
and the sun shone for ten minutes, tear-stained
around midafternoon; here and now
the whole country changes, and
a drab new president has taken office; my
heart beats slowly; breakfast takes a complete silent hour.
These grey skies
are always streaming away over my head-thoughts
into the swallowed east.

Talk is limited to a few words, and those difficult.
Hopes I had yesterday have lost their flavor.
The sky lightens miraculous in one place, darkens
in another.
I recall friends now dead,
(their gravestones, visited in late November or
some January of the mind,
half overgrown with grey grass) how
memory changed them so that they
were caught in one action, in a blaze of spurious light

boring because forever, the multiplicity gone, only
the ikon, the memo, remaining.

There are no ruins here in California.
You feel their lack, in places where otherwise they might
be expected. There are
only ruins of the heart, the
bad taste of an odd dream you had at night
when the rain was falling hard, and
there was to be no coming back of the light.

Only the body shivers, bright and keen
offering some salvation, or at least
the possibility of a slow walk on the breakwater
to observe what changes the late storm has wrought
in the sand (to be wiped away by
little fairweather breakers, and trodden by teenagers).

And now at least it is all clean:
still wet, and with sharp grain-edges from the
storm's baptism: Contemplate
the uninspected, naked self of you, and
listen to the hollowed, odd
distortion of the sea sound, its
infinite spirals, its long meaningless conversations, the
blows of water against water churning on the dead land.

The Process

What is your life composed of?
Sit in a room: the mind is filled. Gently
examine each article.
The places you've been: the
cities are phantoms, they are all
on Sunday, the wind blows through
their walls and their buttresses, the
people are butterflies, moths, the
Mayor is a mouth only, the crowds
are bottoms, genitals, walking in the streets.
The shops are whorehouses, purveying
wares only slightly less aware than their purchasers.

The mountains are clouds of stone.

The trees are chemical factories, with
antennae, like the moth wings of a satellite,
blindly searching the sun.

The colours are a variant of grey. Our
eyes deceive us, their tints are purely subjective.

Our friends, they grow before us in memory;
do you really know what they're like?

A bird sings outside the window. Noise.
Your body contains three engines: food and sex and sleep.
Novels are gossip. Poems are unpleasant to read.

Only in motion, like the cupola of a hummingbird's
ghostly wing, or the mystical track of an electron
or the continuous pattern of music, or

the flash of a smile, the illusion of light
the operations of business, the engagement
of talk, even writing which is one level over oblivion —
only in motion is being.
The room is an explosion of birds
the faces only a shimmer, a
vibration of flesh.
This is a weekday world. God rested on Sunday.

Birth of a First Son

This peace in my flesh is terrible:
compounded of a tiredness I have not felt for years
and force that has brushed me, as
a tape is erased by an immense magnet.

Right here where does one go from now?
Huge things have come and gone.
There was a time when I told God
don't place this thing on me: when
the city lay below under a
fantastic cloud lit by the moon and
I saw everything at once: my
skin crawled and my stomach shook
as if with an unearthly cold or emptiness.
I have felt
a rainbow in my bones, a
white covenant; and in the day
the mountains, ordinarily flat and cut out
of a huge paper, now misted with flowing cloud
and filled with colours, valleys, holes and
enormous glows in the sunlight rifts;
shadows on the plain
brood like an impatient father, the rumbles of an
earthquake that never quite happens;
veils of supernatural rain shift here in dry California
and earth smells of death and birth, the
cactus gasps in it and sends forth spores
I saw the cosmos
in the eyes of my new-born child.

It had always been a life

in which one could, so to speak,
lay up treasure on earth as well as in heaven;
speech conveyed not only meaning but style;
I could pursue ambition and friendship in
the same breath. I have made
many purchases, saying always that
they expressed my spirit, and that compromise,
after all, need only be incarnation.

Now it is different.
I have no axe to grind, and I want
to say exactly what I mean.

What I had mistaken for boredom was
in fact the uncomfortable touch of truth.

Half of living is a desperate, last ditch
defence against boredom. We prefer,
one suspects, to be in pain and interested
than to be all of a sudden without
motive, desire, goals — this
great capacity is great emptiness.
We can stretch until vast things may find a place in us;
what do we do then with the small?

My friends have discovered the elegant; they
avoid large abstractions not only because such things
are intellectually topheavy but also because
they stink of power, they have frequencies
that quickly could burn us out.

They have found
little railroads up mountainsides, have
made tiny photographs of the odd Andes, and

they are not a bit emotional tourists, nor do they
collect the world's chinoiserie in any
but the most generous spirit, nor
have they given up any battle, in fact
they have won the battle of immanence, of
perfect embodiment, of containing the
vast in the small; my problem is
precisely the containment of the dear and small, all
the little things the world is made of,
in the vast.

Keats said: it is the simple flowers of the spring that
I would see again. Gauguin in Tahiti, who had seen
the question of all men, and the gods and the sea,
died with his last stroke
upon 'A Breton Village Under Snow'.

I feel I cannot take up
these particular controls again, nor
ever touch the pulses of a pastoral childhood;
for I do not know whether I control myself
or whether I am controlled by myself. I
have seen a hint of an unbearable freedom.

In the nights I dream that
the house is nearer to the sea in
every hour, and at last
hangs out above a grey and markless beach of black volcanic
    sand.
There is a roaring, and two people who have been
changed by death are singing partsong with
a sweetness I have never heard.

A day is ages long.
In one moment
you can see and hear a thousand things and
there is a tremendous tone, like the after-gonging
of a huge bell whose striking you did not hear —
there is an elemental chord in
every moment, not just
of beauty but of terror also; and
what do you do with all the moments in a day? All that
which properly occupies us, takes a second and a half and
having known that, what fleshing forth
can we bestow on minutes, hours, days?

To be sane it must be possible
for us to be content, most of the time
with secondary goals. At
this point, I have none, there is
nothing more that I desire, and God
seems all too big, and unkind, and
imposing in his kindness when he is kind. He
will not let a baby escape that look of eternity
in its eyes, will not let
a flower escape the implications of its
ringing millioning of molecules and atoms, its
light-years of space between electrons, the
forces in its mass that could move mountains.
He will not let me go except
I bless him, he has taken my sleeve and
it is not interesting at all, in fact dull
but there it is, the world is made
mostly of rocks and undistinguished elements like
silicon and iron, but it is
the world we live on, and dig deep
and there it is. We can do nothing about it.

The Riots, 1968-1969

In these days I hope to find
a little shelter from the blowing wind.
They are too big for me, I sit on the ground
trying to hide from the bright sound.
This candle flutters, here comes the sun
all my night searching is done.
My eyes are black, my head is blind.
They will tear down the walls and let in the wind.
Claws over my ears trying to save
the small patterns that I have.

They came out of the speaker's field
like millions of obscene insects. I
can deal with perhaps three hundred of them
but then it gets too big and dirty and
my throat sucks fear out of the air
and I know my enemy, for I
can see him there.
They marched on the buildings, promising to tear them down.
It was shocking, like a baby in a roomful of adults
or a dead animal on the beach.

Was that your way of getting at me, God?
Did you figure that I was private, and good
and comfortable, and you made the light so
that it would burn off my eyelids?
They are young and have more energy than I. Frequently
they can go to two or three parties in an evening
becoming only gently tired and drunk. I
am vibrated out of kilter, ground out,
spent by such manoeuvres.

Big crowds with one purpose are
like an immense cock, a huge
tumescence clearly visible, bespeaking
gross power, an unhidden purpose.
This gauss they possess, this
involuntary thrust or field
is quite breaking to one of gentle mind.

It wasn't the backstairs, artist-in-jeans,
anarchist bomb and black hat sweet
Kokoshka, Dada, coffeehouse,
enthusiastic girls wearing no underwear
making love to heroes in attics
shooting in the streets sort of affair
or the national, city bell, buildings
draped with banners, state funeral, tanks
and underground presses, overcoated statesmen
tragedy and culture sort of
thing either but
people with blunted faces, minds
full of pot and dull undirected passion
blown up like dead drowned flesh
very desperate, a
shadow all that day over the sun, a
black shade that covered the flagstones like soot
and the trees bloomed crimson sticky flowers
without leaves, with iridescent bark and
my friends were like friends in a dream
whom you daren't approach lest they
become something else, or speak to you
like your mother or start
screaming improbably. In the middle
I spoke to a sad man whom I had some acquaintance with
and the old conversations were broken.

I then wanted to be
in a place with only trees.
A big old cloud, white and fluffy like a sheep
would come up over one mountain and
sail over the next, and the trees
with their sharp pine smell would move
gently in the eternal wind. I
wanted to be safe, having
found one of those seats of moss that
crop up oddly in stones as if meant for us for
always, where a few flies maunder past
and the sun shines hot and clear in
the spaces of the trees and
over the next ridge there would be farmlands and
only a few people who
would run a filling station that also sold
oranges, and beer, and
chocolate, and talk by screen doors slowly
all day till the sun began to fall
and the rivers would be full of water all the year
in deep pools and sphagnum waterfalls and
the sound of gentle rock and wind
water and wood music would stay all day.

I am not given to escaping: given
a fair deal, my friends would not say I am a quitter.
But when the drums and the mad flags come
marching down with always in their faces
and they have so many people with them, all
big and strong, and I believe in words
am an apostle of procrastination and
would rather talk than fight even a committee
this finds me out in my refuge.

What if your light, my God, should
be black to me because I cannot see?
What if your rank smell should be
perfume to those whose nostrils snuff
your real and marvellous air? Should I
go with them, soberly, and with that
awful purpose?

Your epiphanies, my God, are maybe sweet
to your converted, and your poison meat
to those who know their need. My hands
are not so strong, my eyes fail in your lands.
They whose fists now seem uplifted to my head
may be the Satans without whose blessing I am dead.
My fear may make me whole. I still dread
and recognize the pain of my salvation. You
would use other words, another word, but so
I shall understand you. But give me peace
whose ways are strange and whose betrayal is a kiss.

The Third World War

They ask me how I am today?
and I reply a blue jug full of milk.
They tell me that the Westerns and the Lusches
are going on a picnic, and do I want to come?
I inform them how the crabs are eating out my soul.
They stand there, sometimes, kind, embarrassed.
Silence.
I tell them that the world began as a muscle, becomes
a weight marked five pounds, and will end in love.
Mainwaring Warrender was in today with
a cold, said I could borrow his wide angle lens whenever I
     wanted.
I cannot talk to Kelley Hobbs because
he thinks I mean it.
I have been growing a bluish protuberance on my shin
which has begun shedding matter on other peoples' carpets.
They watch it, fascinated, while I speak and
do not notice when I have stopped.
My five trained toads have been getting out of control.
Recently I was stopped in the street by a patrol car which
asked me if I had a licence for them. (There was a
lot of trouble, but luckily I had saved the District
Attorney's life in Africa once.)

Yet I have been
in avenues of green
and golden wands
have brushed my hands
the mists and light
of old Cathay
have covered bright
the great standing sycamore tree

37

this yellow light
of old Pekin
has lit the green
where I begin;
and the music coming from the winter barn
and the steam of the summer byre
and the Christmas blazing of the fire . . .

Wherever your father and mother were
was where you were.
Then later when you moved you carried with you
all the belongings you had packed in your mind.
When the time for the fancy-dress ball
or the interview came, you faced it with equanimity
and you leaned on the wheel of your stopped car
and smoked a cigarette properly, as the ad said you should
and went to church, or did not go to church,
you developed anathemas, you
set up a membrane around yourself, you
did not remember what made you unhappy.

Now when the people say to you
what are you thinking, you think what
kind of question is that, you wish they had rephrased it.
How can you tell them how
the green dragon had just carried you away
in the act of rescuing the damsels that had
hatched from eggs on Mars and
how the lovely negress finally consented
to your argument, and suckled you in pity till
all her garments had fallen from her, and you made love
on banks of marigolds, your doctor's white coat
thrown in the dust, disturbing the butterflies?

You want to save people, but instantly
they have become a meaningful group of
pale blue blocks standing in rows on an empty stage
and the President no longer considers you adviser material.

You found yourself out in a wide valley
where the acid rain passes in sheets and sheaves
over the raindrop grass, glowing with purple haze.
You wandered in the place of skulls and rocks.

All day in the ship they had laboured
cutting up the whale in melon rinds
till at last the evening fell, and your foot slipped
casting you in among the sharks.
Bound to a pagan, you were saved. Later
you clung in the whirlpool to a coffin.

My son is ten months old.
He has learnt to come and
smile at me like a sunflower.
My wife brushes out her long black hair
whenever I feel low.

I shall put on a scarf of leaves and fur
and make friends with the bears.
I shall fell trees for a log cabin
considering how without iron I shall make
latches and hinges, and how without knowledge
of electronics, I shall communicate with other survivors.
I shall conclude a peace treaty with the kites
and persuade the industrious but stupid bees
to share with me their honey, in return for
cultivating flowers.

I shall improvise systems of agriculture.
My tribe will rely on my brown arm.
Mr. Jones and Mr. Loophole will
consult me in certain matters, Mr. Lusch will
depend on my skill, and Mr. Western, though
he cannot read, will be given oral messages instead.

This green and pleasant land
is all the earth there is, all the earth we need.
The caves and vales are balanced by the hills and trees.
The mountains stand upended in the pools.
The late snow lies in the heather, the
early surf runs along the beach like a boy.
Left on the edge of the surge
is a reddened beer-can, bobbing with the wreckage.
Hammered and forged it will make a useful knife.

Over the telephone and upon screens
some kind of life will go on.
Carried by lasers, messages will be improbably received.
In a blue haze, machines will make palaces.

Walking at night, sometimes I see
the interiors of other people's houses.
Their own lamps cast blooms of light and
shadow on their walls. They
have paintings I have never seen, and
beautiful systems for high-fidelity music.
The moon shines on their gables.
They would welcome a stranger.
They must have views of the city that would make me breathe
    with delight.

Come inside, come inside
you have nothing to hide
we have prepared a supper of cold cuts
the wine is on the table, and you have come at last.
After all, you were not so far from home.

I have grown tired.
The table is empty now, the guests departed.
Take your way home, remember
that we saw our way clear to an understanding.
When you meet me in the doorway at another time
do not hesitate, trying to place my name.
How could I possibly be offended?
When we meet again, in the wind or the moon
we will both remember our conversation, both
shout together, 'Didn't I meet you when . . . ?'

Two Poems

If I could touch you with my secret heart
Or warm your fingers with my dearest breath
I would, my love; your coldness is like death
And senseless tissue seals up every part.

If your lips' snow should ever turn to dew
Or your turn ever come again to speak
It could not be my doing. I am weak
Each muscle neither knows nor does what it should do.

In this cold country summer never comes.
In my hands even secrets never keep.
They die, and all their brightness goes to sleep.
Your softness hardens and your touching numbs.

I kill when most I mean to cherish; you
Are my cold queen, despite all I can do.

The circle of Pluto
is dark, and it's old;
But oil-fired deep heating
will keep out the cold.

The Birds

My vision shivers,
a gross pain waits in the wings of my eyes.

I want to go back home.
But the place is blackened, burnt over,
a smell of burnt rubber and turds, the
bleak odour of semen on an old spring mattress.

If I cannot go back I must go forward.
Poetry is so dishonest.
Mostly we wait on the verge, while the
boiling turbulence of pebbles is throttled back,
holding the last surge.
truly, now, you must make love to the dark.

I have been asked to be what I am not.
Really, I'd rather spend life in
white duck sneakers, a butcher-apron sweatshirt,
ankle-pants and a straw hat,
skilled in the sun, believing in nothing,
exercising my mind and my aesthetic sense
on the occasional adulterous love affair.

What does one get out of writing poetry
that one does not get from
committing a spectacular murder or
else playing several vigorous sets of tennis?
Can anyone really love anyone else?
Jesus had it made. He didn't have to be evil.
He could be good-natured always because
he was good natured.

We sat talking all that night
till our faces were swollen and
our lips stung by numb little insects.
Cigarette smoke gulped down like balls of wool.
In the morning we heard the small birds sing
and saw the lights go automatically off.

She is my hero. Helmeted with hair
she goes out into the dark, my chevalier,
my light cavalry, my dancer, she
comes back from scouting, tells me of the progress of the war.
Now she and I lie sick. Her
golden armour's dulled by a blank shine.
My last captain deserted with me in a
bunker, Eva and Hitler, us both
heroes of a noble war.

The air goes bright but it's a lie.
Winter shades are always in the offing.
It must be like this in the
brief summer of Iceland, in the
swift Fall of Greenland, when the icy edge
reminds of Ice-Giants and the last battle of the war
when we all lose, and the black tide
pours over the battlements, and the
banner that we flourish, woven with a flower
thrown down, and grey clouds cover the last
patch of blue;

Come back children, come back old rocking-chair
come back evening, in Oxford, with
red plush blossoms, the white cherry
the buttermilk apple smell of when
it was all all right and nobody missed supper;
come back steamboat, railway train, road map,

44

lonely in places but happy;
come back history. Come back Canterbury
Tales, come back love baby.

Dear body, property of Fred Turner,
with your own odd smell (after exercise
I smell of coffee; after sleep, of brandy left overnight)
with your own dear movements, the juicy soft
clickings of tendons, the duty that you do of
digestion, the breath you continually take, the
honourable heartbeat keeping all in gear,
dear body, dear nature, why do you
kill me with brainsickness, St. Vitus' dance,
this fever that you use to tell me I am
not behaving like myself, the terrible
warnings you give of something going wrong,
the fear you put me in, the savagery with which you
revenge my moral clutchings to be
better than I am, avenge
the death I wreak daily on my own impulses?

I want to be free. I want to
be able to throw everything behind intention.
I want to lead the people into their own happiness.
I want to demand every ounce of torque out of myself
I want to remake the whole world where
men shall not suffer, I want
a different mathematics, so that
two, or three, or many, may be one
I want a world, where nature does not war with freedom
I want a death, and a new birth, in every second.

Back again. I used to walk on the sea shore
on grey days when the sand was sodden;

the ocean turned over like an old blanket
every now and again.
The wind would blow spirals in the rain
the water was cold but kind and gentle.
After a while it would not be so chilly;
a little warmth would gather in the huddle of
myself, and like stacked wheat, which
generates its own surprising heat in crevices,
that smells of whey, and keeps, in its
crust of gold and grey, a ripe moisture,
I would walk sheltered and Bristol-fashion.

I am divided and do not know myself.
I knock on the door. Who's there? Sorry,
you have the wrong number.
Sorry.
Sorry.

If I could only do what I was told
and did not have to blame or praise myself
for every action; if I could take up the yoke
that's perfect freedom, so they say,
if I could love tradition, and if I
could be the beneficiary of some bequest
with lawyers to prevent my every step
and loving aunts to choose my escorts for me
if I were gently ruled, in a way not cruel to my nature
then I could better bear my orphaning.

But we are all alone, you, me, everybody —
(I don't mean this wisely, because wisdom
doesn't seem possible among human beings) —
all alone, uniquely, for we do not share even the *kind* of
    loneliness we bear.
Have pity, that's all. Don't bother me

and I won't bother you.
Spend your life kindly, try to avoid
duties that may make you lie or fail.
Above all be humble. The point of consciousness
is so remotely small, like the
focus of the eye-beam — half a letter on a page —
none of us can think many things at once
nobody when he speaks has much, beyond
a word or two, a feeling, in his head, the
rest is practice, the ease of words oft spoken.
Nobody owns much of time, only this moment,
and it is gone before we knew it came;
nobody has any kingship in the future or the past.

Listen to the birds.
They sing their dainty tunes
without volition, all in the course of duty
keeping their tiny species, so insignificant to anybody,
still in the eye of God.
The rain falls on their perfect feathers. Their
skeletons so delicate (ours are massive)
carry them in their journeys through the air.
They have not learnt not to trust, and their trust
is glorious. Let us watch them, and
since we cannot imitate, bless them at least.
There is so little asked of us.

How wonderful, how wonderful
are all the little corners of the earth!
I watched an inch of ground for half an hour
and every fragment, pine-needle, leaf-mould
dust mote and flower petal —
each fragment had its own shape, its
own colour, and its own shine.

Reflections

The window reflects him looking
out looking in.
He speaks a dead language.
Nobody understands him
they compose their faces
into grimaces
experts of appearance,
they are interested, evaluative, but
nobody is inside.

He is galvanized into strange energy.
Like a dead thing, being
riddled with bullets or shocked by a million volts, he
sits upright, he leaps, he pirouettes like a dancer.
It's me I'm talking about, it's I'm talking about me.
Look in the window, you (me).
What do you see.

The curtain flies apart, the
frame rattles. That is your shape, the
shape of the room, the room you take up.
It's all very precise. The right-angles, the corners
are quite agonizing. I am squeezed to a point.
This is the label saying 'drink me' that I
cannot reach, that you, hoyden, blunderbore, ogre, cannot
edge over with an elbow.
You are a huge vegetable, all marrow, no bone
beginning to rot in the bright summer outside baking
the fetid air within.

From outside he appears like
a man holding a sandwich on one hand

trying to get out of a pair of pyjamas too large for him
while he steps, exactly, with his right foot, onto a thumbtack he
    dropped, yesterday,
with the other.
For such a man the universe is never a proper fit.

The sky creeps up his shoulders, the forces
of his society are tight at the crotch. The earth
pinches his instep, he is vulnerable to everything.
Going into war he finds he's on the wrong side.
He forgets the names of his friends, mislays his glasses
breaks crockery looking for them, changes
down into third on the freeway, looking
vaguely for some ineffable fifth gear.

Looking in the window he sees somebody else,
appalled
for a moment, he sees it's the mailman with
a special delivery package (a pair of
undershorts he left at a friend's).

Into this summer of 1970 I go,
a pirate on dry land, a stout Cortez
discovering once again a Pacific with no boundary.
A mountaineer, I ascend through the foothills, conquer
the upper slopes, find at the summit an ice-cream concession.
In four billion people there's
probably someone who looks, and thinks, and maybe
even has the same name as me.

Conversations: *for Ben Nelson*

How stupid are the facts
the way they slobber at the mouth
the way they sit there fat incompetent
askew like a picture hanging out of true
a sound which has no meaning
the thing shaped not to please the sense
the world a heap of facts garbage
ordure of suns the air and water
of the sickroom the incontinent.
Between the random and the pompous
simply a silly game.

I have been in too many conversations
whose whole point is to obscure the truth
(truth and fact are opposites)
I have heard too many men assert the obvious
as if it had any interest for anybody.

Define your terms in terms of what has been
already defined in terms of what has been already defined in
    terms.
Their language is dead their art
is dissecting the bodies of their friends to find out
what is important about them.

There is no action which is not also a passion.
There is no thought which is not also the screen on which it's
    thrown.

I appeal to the light. So pure it is:
sweetness and swiftness, a child, a cherub
lancing with such innocence, such certainty, through void,

making the blank fact fertile, giving the whole world a constant;
try to catch hold of it, it ceases with such
trust, such submission, it becomes you, it informs you, it
tells you where you are, it warms and comforts you.
like love, whose passage is so swift and absolute
the light is all we have in this world of things.

How tender those conversations we had in Chicago.
For a while the world was not blunted, the time
was not of the clock, but the heartbeat, the syntax
of grace, the lightness of what is most grave;
I have a whole reel of photographs — never came out —
how could you catch onto the rhythm or stop the process —
I have a dance in my mind now, whose step
has not faded yet.
How aware the agreement (not based on any
tiresome old bandwagon, the bandwagon of rhetorical,
dictionaried and forced, totalitarian, moral inperialism)
— an agreement based only on itself, fed
and ennatured by our readiness.

'The sweetness of life', the balance of silence with speech,
the caracoles, frescoed baroque of pure ornament
that nevertheless holds up with its filigrees
roofs that keep out the cold and the rain: we were
caryatids, angels with blazing eyes and wings as natural
as arms.

It's all an illusion, just as reality is —
an electronic whisper that carries from one side
of the universe to the other, like speaking in a dome;
it's all an illusion, a precious, warm,
well fed, morally indefensible illusion, the
crazy rebellion called civilization, the argument

blessing the facts and wounding them, making them torches;
seeing their emptiness, making their emptiness full.

(Philosophy, losing its children, the sciences and
the humanities, has, like an impotent mother, turned
frigid and hard. Sterile and elegant, dressed
in the latest fashion, sipping a cocktail, selecting
an occasional peanut from the dish, her legs crossed,
her thoughts full of teeth, she watches,
hotly, with dark circles under her eyes, with
a yearning and vicious jealousy, the flirtations of her children.

Her obedient foetuses, the ones that never got born,
repose like little white ghosts behind her forehead. Their
unformed and pathetic genitals, maimed and torn, still
ooze a faint ichor.)

Outside, in that spring, the amazing spring of Chicago
all the green buds were unfolding. It was
all green and grey, a softness hung in the air like a mist
containing gently all of the furls and the balance of leaves.
The city stood stoutly, absurd with an amiable absurdity
in all its civilian virtue, its mercantile pout, like
a rich man about to step on a banana.
In the trees though, carried by that unearthly air
rococo blossoms and squirrels like *putti* were playing.

The Garden of Eden

To describe Eden is the easiest thing to do
and the best. All the expected
should be there in their places, the leopard, the
white lamb, the albino oxen, the fruit-bearing trees.
The detail is tiny. In each leaf
the veins are passionately clear.
The dragonflies, divided into genuses
hover above the slipping water; the roots of the turf
are sodden with water, the thin moon
has no fear of the midday sun, but stands in the blue black.
We see them, coming from behind the oak trees,
for the first time, childish and wise, with
the grace of models, their body hair
shining in the shafts. Adam and Eve.

Time goes slowly.
There was the incident of the serpent, quickly forgotten.
Nobody is going to die.

Portrait of the Artist

I am becoming longer, more substantial.
I surprise myself in a mirror, having
such grace and seriousness, I
must be developing a personality, someone
you could parody, a figure in a play.

I have got fatter but wear clothes with more panache.
My house has been burgled, I share
the imposing material vulnerability of the middle class
or of parents when you were young, who
saw to everything, even had disasters, but
who were so competent and
huge in the world's horizon that nothing could befall them.

I wear glasses and display my own tastes in personal manner.
I am contented and usually find things amusing.
I have become conscious of slights and bad manners.
I am still, however, astonished.

As a woman, who, bearing a child,
is made over totally to a system
inherent in her genes, so we mature
along lines that cannot be denied. But still
my commonsense is so absurd . . . !

The Water World

Release from pressure:
into the cold soft shadow
everything brighter, brightly, into the
blue world, all away in a dive
cold and salt, it is clear in itself
needs to reveal nothing. Naked. Into
the eve-shadow, limelight, our first stage.
Almost you can breathe through your skin;
tiger-world fishes, their girth carried
by tiny cherub wings;
the angelfish, winged wheels.
In the rock hideaways, the crabs
lurk, uncarapaced, growing new plates.
Clomp! goes a bubble.
Breathing is like a long drink of fresh water.
It goes down right inside you, clear
down to the groin, it tightens up
the skin about the breastbone, its
pleasure is heady.

Lying by a blue sound
every ounce of flesh and fat
yielded to the lassitude of gravity
your whole life going in a straight line
you see the white moon in the blue sky
like a florin at the bottom of a pool.
If you dare to look
the sun is a pink splash with a heart of gold.
Eyes flicker, drop, close; tears
wrinkle the nose-horns, mouth waters.
A sigh of wind blows back the grasses.
It smells of sweet tobacco, tears, and rum.

The sea's as black as asphalt, newly laid,
before the roller, absorbing light,
giving it all back in a loose splash like a diamond.
Lying there you lose your balance
the world topples, rides. It's
so safe though, it carries you wherever it's going.

On a rainy day
Mist down close to the flowers
earth teeming with runnels
a rush of drops from the tree
the roar of impacts all over the world
quite taken from yourself, undisturbed
with one chief silence, whose other voice is sound
you carry with you a home of your own
made of instants of rain, a packed tent of falling
you inhabit the space with your shape
your refuge is a broad-leaved sycamore
your nakedness to the wet is your only defense
your values are the taste of rainwater
the smell of mint and rainwater, the smell of leaves,
you move within like a clockwork toy, or a
sundial casting a rain shadow; you breathe
the pattern of the air, you hear the patter of the rain.

Asleep, you wake to another day that has not come yet.
The darkness is a bath of air,
The birds are all dormant,
hiding their heads under their wings,
You think of all the friends that you have known
you hear a jetliner inch past above
filled with tired people, up there in the almost morning sky.
Almost morning.
Where do the small animals sleep?

Sage smell where there is no breath of wind.
Crickets and frogs
gradually tune out.
The hemisphere
planted with stars like a great map
waits and is empty.
You see it first behind you, in the west:
the shapes welling up out of the greyness, a whale-shaped hill,
a flower button, starred in its centre, six inches away.

In your pèlerinage, weltwanderung,

your sharing, turning over the earth
you find in a shell the history of the sea.
If wafts up out of the holes, the waiting places
the interstices, fire glowing out of a crack
when the dead hearth shifted, the dead heart moved.

In the line of the vortex, speckled with brown,
the spiral spotted with pink (the white exterior caked with
    chalk)
you hear the blood of your hand, and see
with the redness of closed eyes,
the blush of your flesh held up to ward off the sun.

In this house
sitting in the bone-warm haze
surrounded by wood and cloth
there is no need
to say anything or
do anything.

I think I may stay
like this, for ever.
It is total. I
think I may sleep and be awake
both at the same time in
this fixed power,
this perfect possibility;

but that I know that the thought
pursued far enough, will lead
me on to discontent, the
light of the room will darken, the
fire cool or become uncomfortable.

All my history has come up
and is standing around me.
Not the surface play of fact and event
but the deep stream, the
myths of flowers and loves, the
emerging competence of feeling,
the sense of change, the sense
of the field of change;

as a boy I
would sometimes feel the world as a totality, a single note,

my awareness penetrating the walls of my room
and in a shaken, mystic excitement
I could see the shadow of the world's turning, the
coasts of reality, its contours, I
could breathe the space between atoms,
I felt extraordinarily free in those times;

This time it is like music
with the tang of honey and the thick pluck of cream.
It is very subtle.
I am hand in hand
with all my lost friends.

Now, like the soft crack
of wax, my skin awakes, feels
its everyday texture.
The fire has coated one side with sweat.
I must decide whether to move, to
change the record, or
to try to bring my stasis back;
so lazy
in my warm room I must decide to choose.

Tochter aus Elysium

He is still there.
Though I stole his knowledge, beat him at chess
(sitting in his white halls under the fanlights, the
pieces made of black and silver steel)
and even, in the last stages, betrayed
him with his wife, myself the tempter, knowing myself
to be evil, persuaded her away from his superior wisdom;
though I carried her away in the night, and
in the morning watched for his pursuit;
though we fought at last, under the
huge elm trees in the everlasting cornfields; and I strangled him;
though I never buried his body, he
is still there.

I became a jet-setter; more and more
I discovered how alien was my stolen sweetheart;
our conspiracy based on escape became
only a memory, stirring
vestiges of a ruined intimacy.
We were beautiful before strangers, charming
them gracefully, united in
the choice of the wine and the
artists we bought to impress them; united only in that;
for after all she
still has the purple iris, the nailless toes, and
the birth scar of the star-dwellers and her
dead mate comes back in both of our dreams;
and, though
she has become thoroughly trivial, sometimes
high in the mountains or
confronted with virgin snow she
weeps without knowing it: and we will never have children.

Do you remember one of the paintings of Chagall –
the one with the cow jumping over the moon, and the cock
and other symbols of a diminished objectivity, parables
of disrupted time?
In the night sky, with azure and crimson
like the glow of a heart, the colours
that float over eyes that are closed, the
colours of darkest night, there are lovers
asleep in the clouds, with her cheek
like the cheek of a blush, resting
so gently, a snowflake, on her lover's (a
peasant's, a hedge-boy's face, with a badger's mysteriousness).

I forget where we saw it, somewhere in
Switzerland perhaps, where we lunched with the novelists,
talked about Swiss education and cultural decline,
despised the Germans, and so on.

Marya (that's what we called her – the real name
like the née of the radium woman, quite unpronounceable)
told me how sometimes her husband
and she were like that, in the picture. I
shrugged, in a gesture of mine, adjusting the
tie between coat-breasts of tweed, turning
away;
I feel like a donkey servicing a mule.

The government's still keeping tabs on her; there's not
much left for their scientists to discover, dissecting
the marvellous ship that they came in. They
phone her, sometimes, late in the night
to ask if she knows of some principle,
symbol, or sign, to help their enquiries. Lately
she's forgotten nearly all of it. I took down on tape

61

all that was relevant, long ago, when
he was my friend, taught me everything.

But last night I heard him again! in an inn
I caught sight of his face, its pallor
flushed with the fire, the young men
and girls, in sweaters and casts (their skis
stuck in the opal snows, lit to their depths by the windows)
sitting around him, hearing his wisdom.
I didn't believe it.
Marya went in to him. I
sat on a stone. That night
there was an awful thaw, the hills became green
and the sun rose again, in the west, with the moon
like a cave, hanging beside him
and the sky clotted with lovely blood
packed into tiny bright billows of cloud, and
there was a huge sound, like a gong, and
the sun and the moon set again, wild
odours of spring, of hay and of apples
blew through the streets (reporters
from all over the world came next night, but nothing whatever
    happened).

I sat on a stone, remembered
how in my high-hoped dream
I'd imagined my journey, my calling, the
spaces of sky, the American Rockies, the
dawns in American passes, the road
spearing like light through the foothills:
the valley:
blue like a smoke
lying, the naked, the promised, the veil of the mist
the river, with frogs and with fishes

wet in the dank, in the dawn, in the shadow
the banks of the current, rich with black mud, the
coconut trees, the Japanese trees with bent branches
their feathery leaves, the birds not awake yet;
my valley, sent me by God
where I'll toil at the dams, and sink
my wrists deep in the mud, making nests
for the flowers and fruit-trees.

Remembering my betrayal, I wept
in the wound that you feel when you're
caught out, and sly and diverse
misused the kindness of a friend.
Breaking the Christmas present, on the first day.
Such things are so hopeless, nothing
can ever assuage them.

My land is now
a conditional place, a suburb of no great city
where the views are pretty enough. I'm so lost.
My Mary never came back to me
(though it's a matter of doubt, consulting my journals, whether
I could ever call her mine);
the fortune I made is now
tied up in the courts, and I'll never see it again.
My friends, whom I see to play poker on Saturdays
never believe in my stories. I'm
far too young, so they say, to have been through so much.

In the nights I relive parts of my past.
Sometimes it rises like dew, and I weep
with the pain of the loss, and at times, even,
transported and blissful, a Bernini mystic
a little baroque, perhaps, but my sighs are quite genuine:

Sometimes I see
the whole pattern, laid out
like a flight path behind me, blue lights and a cross
of white neon, with the rain of a storm.

The Actor to the Audience

Do you want me to take your hand, shaking
slightly, and lead you into an inner world?
Or would you rather I did as I did last year, lying
prostrate, inviting you to cut me to pieces, peer
into my heartland, tread me with your boots,
the weakest of creatures, shrinking from your contempt? And
  you,
coming to hear my story, amateur psychologists.

Why should you know my secrets?
Perhaps I should rather be
a mask of worked bronze, in a haze
of sparks, an insufferable elegance standing
in the heart of my cool world, surrounded
by perfect figures, isosceles or hyperbolic
an obelisk at rest under a windy blue blue sky.
Perhaps in your vulgarity you should take me for a god.

I am not a priest. You would sense this, for you are
not only parasites, lice on my body, but
very discerning, you even love me in your way.
Should I be matey? your buddy, going bowling,
on the town, sinking a beer and commenting on the girls' legs?
It is far too late for that, for you see
you have already discovered my weaknesses.

Perhaps I should assume your indifference.
You came here to this place on the off-chance
that there should be some small epiphany, or to
see what our kind looked like, or out of boredom,
or to acquire knowledge, or to provide subjects for later
  conversations.

I am resolved into the supplicant.
You are my masters, my mistress. Really I'm
trying to get back into your company, to rediscover
what you never lost, the sense that the one on the seat beside
   you
is just as you are. My condescension is despicable.
I have left you no way out, except to leave.

The Proposal

When we got off the plane there were no delays.
We were whisked into the city (Magnolian
the tycoon, who is only twenty-seven,
had sent a car);

In the evening we sat in his gardens
waiting for him to fly in from Seattle.
he arrived late, having showered and changed
in his club, not wanting to see us in his
business suit: he had on
a waistcoat of pearl, and a huge tie, an
English sports coat; we would dine in the city;
meanwhile there'd be cocktails.

Faye was joking about last summer, how
we threw him in the fountain;
I remembered the bells of that city
under the sun of the Mediterranean;
The moon already rising now, the clouds
violet and stretched up there in the deep sky (remarkably
free of the smog for this time of year).

They threatened to leave without me: I put down
The *l'Oeil* I'd pretended to read: can I
approach him with this?

We ate at the *Papillon.* I paid the check.
Later we walked by the harbour. Faye
became silent, knowing what I must say.
At last he asked me what I was doing, so far
from my musical scores, my slide-rule and my Big

Mama computer, how could I bear
leaving New England this time of the year?
— just to disturb an old friend?

I didn't say anything: hailed a taxi
told the half-asleep driver to take us crosstown
and up to the hilltop boulevard, where the
great dome of the telescope, the ball of an eye
echoes, for those who are interested, that of the
Hall of State Justice one mile below;
Vlad was impatient; in the end
we stood on the parapet talking, and I put forward the plans.

Faye stood a little way off; her perfume and cigarettes glowed
    in the dark.
When I'd finished she stepped on a grating
breaking the heel of her shoe.

He could not commit the Magnolian system to such a great risk.
There were factors: the cost, and the public relations.
He was already corrupted, he said, trying to make light of it; he
    put on a frown;
he was flattered; said that he'd help with his own private
    fortune.

I looked up at the dome; lit with dumb irony my last cigar.
The driver slept in his taxi. If he only had eyes to see,
I was thinking, how clear it would be!
Morning was near; the sphere of the sky held us safely;
guarded the sleep of the city with arms of its own.

The Cave

As a rationalist, I have always believed there
must be some heresy in any system of philosophy.

His argument was couched in subtle terms.
All the birds of the air and the fishes, and
the gentle beasts, and those whose behaviours
are irascible, and the stemmed and leaved things,
the mechanics of stones and histories,
the many cultures, each with their own
set of organs, their feedbacks, ironies, self-
evaluations, were his argument. He
left me with little to ground my discourse on, Monsieur Satan,
(for it was he); there was evidently no area of disagreement.

I was impatient. How can I
wait for my damnation? The time may never be ripe.
After all, I'm young, the goliards
may have left the beer-halls in this part of the country
and gone over the hills, the garlands at the door grown withered
    and the girls grown up into
aprons and children, before you will let me be ready;
the age may have passed, the emperor's concubine
sent away to the northern barbarians, singing
her suicide song, the nightingales
displaced by a change in the wind-belts, this
pleasant parkland drifted with dust from the icecap
the palaces empty and smelling of urine, graffiti
on the walls before I can come home.

He kept me in his study, drawling
his words, selecting at times
a text from the shelf to score down his points.

I drummed in frustration, offered my arm for his scalpel
got up and walked about, admitted
all kinds of foul things of myself.
Clearly he did not want my soul.
Doing business was different, he said, in a credit economy:
it was a question of waiting and negotiation.
He steepled his fingers, told the secretary to show me out.

The western drift of this cavern where I live once
yielded gold and amethysts. They
left me here some weeks ago, promising
to get help, and have not returned.
Both feet have swollen beyond repair. I eat
what the strange little people bring me, twittering
in their own language, scared, with huge,
sightless eyes. My visions have increased in frequency:
l'ivresse des grandes profondeurs.
Sometimes I imagine myself to be the walls
looking in at myself: sometimes it seems
that the mountain is all that there is, with its
unspeakable weight, and the cave
is its only bubble, containing the whole of the world.

I have become fascinated with my few belongings.
My tin cup, which I keep at the waterfall;
my worn wooden bowl, which the small people
religiously fill every few hours with saffron and rice; my
    compass
of rich white metal, the needle floating on oil,
its direction hopelessly deflected by huge masses of iron.

In my dreams I am always
Suited and formal, in boardrooms and cocktail parties.
One night there was an exquisite red wine

served at a dinner, from a valley in France
full-bodied and genial, meaty, like a warm fire
or a fabric so heavy and deep that it comforts the soul.
And the silver made mists on the cambric!
— I even remember the stitching on my shirt-cuff, the
shadow cast by the candle lying along the cheek of the
lovely red-headed lady in green sitting beside me, the
Principessa —

They told me when I came into this country
to beware of the caves. On the south slope
Of the mountain there are goatherds in summer. In autumn
they make fine cheeses and dance on the threshing-floor:
their language is cognate with Greek.
The limestone, they say, is what gives the country wine its
    flavour.

I cannot wait any longer!
I must make another appointment with my gentleman scholar
    the
devil — curious how far apart are his eyes —
to see if he can get me out of here, damned
and delivered, supported by clean white bandages, my
maimed feet healed, only a trace of a limp!

They will surely say I have been talking to myself.
The strong young men with their backpacks and lederhosen,
the expedition psychologist with his pipe, they
will question me closely, nodding at one another.
They will not notice the footprints in the sand.

Those heroes, with their raisins and chocolate, their
maps and canteens, will never find me here.
Perhaps in a thousand years I will become the core of the

        volcano, the
outer cliffs bursting apart in fire, the
white, actinic light pouring
in shafts though the stone made transparent,
the people of the village running in terror
burnt by the radio-carbons, the curious
spectrums of isotopes, skin cancers and
genetic diseases.

They have kept me here for the safety of the community.
That is why they will not grant my requests.
But they do not know how hard it is to wait.
Still, in the centre of my mountain
I spin my heresies. I do not ask much.
I would behave myself, and eat human food.
I would catch up with my friends
who play their guitars under hedges and who
beg under inn signs for their bread, who on feast-days
have honey and cream, young girls bring strawberries,
cheeses and wine. I would make no disturbance.

In Venice

It was a failed honeymoon.
Venice of white marble *fletynge in the large see*
A Botticelli model but with a bad twist in her eye.
It rained for four days.
The Grand Canal, as Helen said, is like
the line of contact between two gloved hands
wrestling with each other, or like, in a mirror,
the huge bent 'S' in the signature of William Shakespeare —
does a canal, bridged how you will, divide or unite?
— or is it, he says, an entity of its own — quiet now,
opaque and milky like an amniotic bath or
the heavy wash of sperm — is it no dividing line
but an intelligence of itself? Is a man
a sperm's way of making another sperm?
Venice is a city of suicides; do they cut their veins
and bleed in that water like a senator?
Do they die on the best days, when it is all blue, or
when, like this, the canal is empty save for a barge or two
laden with rotted fruit? — when the rain makes circles
and awnings drip, and swells push at the walls
and beat into crumbling doors, their panels
split and weathered with the white salt?
The silence is sinister here.
They sit together in the back of a launch, whose captain
they have given no instructions.

They have passed the grotesque bulk of
San Giorgio Maggiore, and directly astern is
Santa Maria di Salute, with its domes. On bright days
the whole place dances like a dervish, the little flags
and cupolas of San Marco blaze with a feverish light,
like the light of Constantinople, or the loess yellow glow

of Pekin — there are red ragged silks hanging from windows.
— It's not like Italy at all, you know.
— the food isn't fresh.
— the floods were just as bad as Florence.
— nobody noticed.
— sometimes the water is pure river water, from the Po.
— was Marco Polo a Venetian?
— Desdemona was, but Cassio was a Florentine.
It's the edges that are worst.
At a certain point every system reaches some quantum
    completeness,
every harmonic included, so it acts on the world as a whole.
This never becomes total, except in Venice.
— We left the car in the Piazzale Roma. Damn. I
forgot my camera.
— You shouldn't let moods affect you like that.
— The place is like a huge mask. I feel paranoid.

It's like a mask, with many noses and breasts,
made for the celebration, once only, of a sacrifice; left
like the head of Orpheus, to float out to the islands.
The horizons are terrible. There should not be so much water.
The clouds, on the sunny days, build up into Christian palaces.
In the evening, after a day of rain, the sun
squeezes out crosses. There is nothing that is not emblematic.
The water turns horribly pale, the cedars peer out
from over the walls of the cemetery, San Michele is lonely;
the island itself is completely artificial, and is made
in the shape of a rectangle.
Each bridge appears to be final.
— They're like Japanese bridges.
— Japan is the other frontier.
— What do you mean?
— I was thinking of San Francisco. Suicides

always jump off the land-side of the Golden Gate bridge.
— It would take too much resolve to jump off the other side.
(bridges in Japanese films are always symbolic of
deaths, or of edges.)
— Venice is all edges. The city divides the water, the water
    divides the city.

They were both virgins, and still are, though
the sheets on the first night were bloody.
After a week they don't talk any more.
She is a pale, freckled, English girl. She smiled at me very
    briefly.
He, though his back was turned to me, had
the slab-sided cheeks of a police chief.
I saw them in a café, across a tiny, rain-swept
piazza. Their story is certainly untrue.

The Frontiersman

Chicago in 1895. Clarissa Armour,
whom I came to know later when she was very old
leans like a lovely wraith in her Egyptian
peacock silk: she is very white, a triangle face
huge eyes, and a decided, if languid
manner. She has large pale lips and
has been trying to persuade herself in this Tiffany room
(the *New Art Club* and *Lysistrata* on the table)
which of her young men she will marry.
One is romantic and rich, and the other
is poor but honest. She is broad of body
has breasts of white that, unsupported, fall
heavily within her gown. And she is tall.
She has half fainted, we see now, across a simple sofa.

As it turned out, she married neither, and is still
technically speaking, an old maid.
The family was disturbed. Large sums
were missing, to be found invested most unwisely
in silver mines and schemes for solar power.

Clarissa had met Zeke, Mad Ezekiel MacNab, a man
whose powers of persuasion, claimed the *Chicago Star*
were matched by his deceitfulness alone. Poor Stanford,
one of her suitors, was the Pinkerton who bared the fraud.
He was astonished she could love such a man. Zeke
was not handsome, and much below average height.

Ezekiel Hamish MacNab was a photographer,
one-time snake oil agent, a fair painter, with a genius
for weak investments and weaker investors.
He had travelled the Chisholm Trail, and had been everywhere;

Rajahs remembered him; Geronimo was his friend;
lynch-mobs desired the pleasure of his acquaintance.
State congresses knew his name.
He owned one of the earliest automobiles.
Clarissa maintains that she was faithful to him all her life
though he died in 1900 from a tar and feathering.

His famous painting of the Grand Canyon
is his masterpiece. The background, rosy stone, is
accurate in detail, and has been used by
geologists at Caltech, calculating changes in
the Canyon's landforms in the ninety years between.
In the painting it is evening. He has placed
a huge, impossibly snowy mountain on the horizon;
the sky is blue and gold. On the plateau's brink
there are feathery, romantic trees, arbutuses and xerophytes:
All the edges are softened by the glow, although this
has been attributed to his astigmatism.

But in the trees there is a crazy profusion of birds!
Perfectly observed, there are Scarlet Tanagers, and Thrushes,
Finches, Robins twice their normal size,
Buntings, and Bluebirds, and Tyrant Flycatchers;
there is even an extinct Moa, and a Kiwi, and
an Egyptian Ibis in profile, with perfect feathers.
They are set out on twigs and on the ground like
an ornithological illustration: above them, flying,
is a Crane or Heron, half pink with the falling sun,
half in vague black against the sky. There are ill-omened
Swallows, each with a perfect bright eye. The artist
has captured a Peacock also, strutting near the edge
with a slightly hysterical bounce in its step.

In the foreground can be seen the tools of the artist's trade.
A heavy camera, on its tripod, with a huge hood;

a box for the large frames that must be inserted;
a camp-chair, and tent, with a bowler hat on the pole
(the picture can be viewed in the Chicago exhibition);
to one side is the artist himself, the paint still
apparently fresh, depicted in swift, cartoon strokes;
Before him is his easel, and on it simply
a grey wash, and near the centre, an enormous eye.

Another peacock, that we do not see at first, has almost tripped
   him.
His self portrait has a huge nose that slaloms down over
his tiny, lugubrious moustache; he has no chin; one
or two pimples are hinted. His eyes are oddly large and
   beautiful, with
long black lashes. MacNab was the originator of the phrase:
   'never give a sucker
an even break', which he used to say with
a Scottish accent, rubbing his hands;
it shows in his face. In the picture
he is putting the finishing touches on his elaborate signature;
He is dressed like a cartoon congressman, with a string tie.

We catch him, just about to step back
from his work, with the fantastic
evening sun upon him. The whole painting
is a riot of soft colours and meticulous details.
Many did not believe he had been there at all;
others migrated west
because of his inspiration, and found the Grand Canyon a
   disappointment.

Clarissa, who funded him for five years, died last week.
She was still pale, but wore black in her later days,
not blue as she had done in her youth.
She said it suited her better, though I
will always remember her in peacock blue.

The Search for Tom and Lucy

For Missy and Gary Albers

It is the target
that sucks the thrifty arrow down to a point.
Whatever he had said to her, or she to him
it was all one. In the motel,
in the parlour of her father's house, in the
early morning before anyone was up,
on the huge hill over the breathing Pacific,
even after the plane trip, he
was now giving with the
exuberance of an oil well; oh, and she
was so full of animal spirits even
an inch of her skin spoke nude. The freckles
were swamped with her blush: she would
mottle with a touch, and like linen
cloth scorched almost from the dryer, smelling
clean, would burn in his hands for a moment.

They could be dry or sweat gently, it seemed at will.
Each carried a molten core about inside.
They were struck by the differentiation of their organs
the curious volutions, grotesque petals
the dew distilled from them, water on a duck's back,
swan's neck, in sleep hiding its head under its wing.

Everything for days felt like feathers. They
would get *tremor cordis,* separately, would
forget each other for a moment, like a child
who on Christmans Eve must forget, when he sleeps.

And the poem goes no further.
We do not know them, and if
they should be seen by you or me they

would be blank, having surnames, and
surely would not recognize us.

There was a couple who
lived in Marin County for a while
who are likely candidates, but a check of their records
makes positive identification impossible.

It is a question of privacy. I have walked
on their hill, a dwarf, in its sages and poppies, the
whole rough, hairy thing sloping down to the coastal forest.

There is a place
where you can see thirty-five valleys, some
with mist in them, with redwoods in the mist and
mushrooms in their root-moulds;
and a cold saddle that bears snow
in early spring, a wind from the uplands,
eaves of the forest a hundred yards away.

(When they were here
it was to oversee the tearing out of the railroad tracks:
there were gangs of men in the dark
before dawn, with mattocks and spades. Nobody spoke.
Breath, as it never does in a dream
steamed in the arc-lights.)

I also saw the house in San Francisco
where one of them once lived.
It has changed, and the grocer downstairs
has retired, gone to live in San Diego
with his cousin from Canton.
There were telephone numbers on the wall in the lobby
all of them recent. The search

has turned up some interesting stories:
it was like looking for virgins in second-century Rome.

I have a blurred photograph,
a sense of humour, and periodic headaches.
Sometimes it seems
as if I am trying to push a string.
I was not meant to be a detective.
It occurs to me that
if they had a history, it would destroy them.
In this cast I would be father time,
the local draft-board, a
little man in an overcoat, even
perhaps an agent whose mission is to find them, catch
them, and transport them back across the iron curtain.

What seemed always so shocking about them
was their freedom. He
was capable of extraordinary, and good-humoured
violence. She had decided that
she could do anything at all, it was like
winning a first prize and being allowed
to take home all one could carry from a great department store,
    or
like, in a dream, flying, or having found
a urinal, no longer needing to look for one.
This is quite serious. If you think about it
you will see what I mean.

Really all that the people I represent
are asking for, is a happy ending.
They want to know if it lasted, and if so, how. As for the lovers,
their gorgeous defence is purely a logical trick, they

have reversed causality, and I shall never find them.
Still I can tell you the kind of stockings she wears,
the place on the heel of his shoes that is worn down
from his impatient walk; his habits with small change;
her fetish for expensive handbags; his satirical gift;
her exquisite tastes, his music, her finely sharpened pencils.

But who can pluck back the arrow to the bow?
What subtle pencil can retrace
the smoke back to the steamer in the bay, into
its smokestack, down to the rage within?
Who can verify what hasn't happened yet?
Look into the air they yet perhaps will breathe, the
scentless scent of poppies and of sage still under the ground:
the air serves only now to see things through;
the scent, perhaps, tells all there can be told.

Libbard's Last Case

The last three miles were quiet
and unspeakably fragrant. The scream of
the train, and the crashing gears
of the bus faded out of his ear.

One must walk over the ridge.

The great detective, his last case closed.
This is the village where
he spent his terribly brief honeymoon many years ago.
(They shot her in the gravel pit after
two hours of nervous, distracted bargaining. Libbard
lost her because of an unprofessional mistake.)

The cart track winds between meadows.
There is the strange scent of the dandelion
fresh and dry, like a girl's hair newly washed.
The grass is shiny. Blackberries roll on its blades.

He comes down the hill to the village.
An old man, who must be Zebedee, has just
untied the flat-bottomed punt and is pushing it out
among waterlilies.
Over in the great east field the
barn is almost full. Later
that evening Libbard will walk out there
as he used to, under a moon peeling through
ancient white clouds.
A few drops of rain will patter in the dark.
He will take shelter, sitting on a hay-bale.
He will smell the smoke of the autumn burning.

Earlier that fine evening
he greets Mrs. Shippen with politeness and gallantry.
He can stay as long as he likes, in the loft bedroom
with its big cloth chairs and
mothballs in the wardrobe.
The stairs creak as he comes down for supper. He
limps a little, for it is that time of year.

In the morning he sees someone
among the elms, with a bow, slipping from trunk to trunk.
He thinks nothing of it, for he is retired.
The stairs creak as he goes down to breakfast:
tea, the newspaper, and rashers of bacon.

The country, overnight
has gathered its energies, burst into a still
deeper, more buzzing glow. Like a
golden blush, the fields have ripened and blaze
in the new mist, grain netted with grey.
The birds rise to a shout, and are silent
leaving the lark only, sharpening his juices in the blue.

Fishing in the millpond later that day, Libbard detects two
    figures
gesticulating on the further bank. One is a girl.
He decides to have nothing to do with it.
A dark shade comes over the day, there
is a cello in the flutes, the warbling is timorous of thunder.

The afternoon is rainy. He
goes to his room early, with a good novel and a pint of whisky.

The next day Briscoe, his recent assistant,
comes on a visit, overweight and puffing,

raincoat over his arm. Libbard
never liked Briscoe: the man was ambitious.
He gives him the slip, leaving him
playing at darts in the Seven Stars.

Later he sees the man with the bow again.

On the hill over the village, near the gravel pit,
the girl of the millpond meets him with a message.
She has a lovely wisp of hair over her eyes,
freckles, a short coat. She thinks
someone is trying to kill her brother.
Libbard buckles down. That night
one of the bulldozer men working on the atomic pile
three miles on the far side of the woods, is found
with a grey goose arrow under his second rib.
The old story of Cain, says the detective
to himself; the film flickers for a moment,
going into the next reel.

But the illusion does not waver.
The third day blooms like a nosegay,
a little wind has sprung up and the
air carries the sound of the cock,
the weir changes its note every second,
the sun burns the fine skin under the eyes and whitens his hair.
All over the fields,
almost throughout the county, a late-blossoming weed
locally known as Lady's Dowry, has come out —
its scent is heady like honey; it forms
echelons of stars, each hedge is a milky way.
The bees are hysterical, one or two children have been stung.

Libbard has been up to the big house
on the rise over the river. He sips
sherry with the master, whom he knew at John's.
He has plenty to go on now, Jessica's
brother is in danger, two men must be watched.
A huge liver-coloured Labrador bitch
lolls in the corner.

The wind drops. Evening odours descend from
the paper-handkerchief-tree, a hundred feet high
as they walk in the grounds.

On a rich hot night, in the rose-garden
the story reaches its climax. There are shots, and a chase.
An arrow transfixes his derby; satanic motives
come to the surface, a cottage is searched
to reveal the psychotic ritual.
In the moonlight the roses appear to swell, there
is a chuckle from a waterbird settling in the pool, black,
with its broken statuary.

In the morning Libbard must leave, for he has
a sick aunt in Highgate. His part was played by himself.
Mrs. Shippen is Mrs. Shippen. Briscoe
who is a loose end, was played by Briscoe.
The Master, who is a real person, has asked
that his name not be used.
Jessica is an actress. Her brother
does not exist for the purposes of the story,
for he never appears.
Any resemblance is purely coincidental.
There is no such plant as Lady's Dowry.
The labrador bitch came from another story altogether.